CONCEPTIONS

and *images* :

Pro-life poems

with

PRISONERS' PARDONS'

Revised

together with related poems,
including those
originating in courts and jails.

James Howard Trott

2015

OAK AND YEW
PRESS

CONCEPTIONS

and *images* :

Pro-life poems

with

PRISONERS' PARDONS,
1st edition   1992; 2nd edition 1993; 3rd edition 1998

Revised 2015

together with related poems,
including those
originating in courts and jails.

James Howard Trott,

copyright 2015
James Howard Trott

Oak and Yew Press
Philadelphia

OAK AND YEW
PRESS

Introduction

The poems collected as *Prisoners' Pardons* were originally dedicated to men and women who had gone to prison for their faith demonstrated in self-sacrificing and peaceful actions on behalf of "the least of these" Christ's brethren, the yet-to-be-born. Those poems were offered as a request for pardon for us not in prison with them.

I remain convinced the greatest barrier to stopping abortion is the church's refusal to set aside its idols of material well-being, personal comfort and reputation before men. The abortionist murders and the F.A.C.E. bill added further impediments to the godly activity known as "abortion clinic rescue". (The F.A.C.E. bill is a classic "bill of attainder"). History may prove that large movement was a seed that died to the end of growing a greater tree.

Thus the current collection of poems is intended more broadly as an encouragement to all pro-lifers, in all the many capacities in which their sacrifices are made, and secondarily as a rebuke to all who love the highest seats in our churches, but refuse to the take up Christ's cross for the innocent unborn. Babies die all around us, yet the church fattens itself in this day of slaughter. God grant us repentance.

Writing about abortion is difficult. Words on this subject have long been substituted for active obedience so that all words have become suspect. It is particularly difficult to write poetry about this horror because a poem requires some abiding redemptive element -- and there is nothing redeeming about the deliberate killing called abortion. We pray and labor to be delivered from these child sacrifices made on the altars of the world's idols.

Jim Trott
Philadelphia   4 July 2015

CONTENTS

SECTION TWO: POEMS 1967-1988:

SECTION THREE: POEMS 1989-2015

SECTION FOUR: JAIL POEMS (1988-1997)

SECTION ONE: *PRISONERS' PARDONS*

I.   HEARERS NOT DOERS

FAT CITY

We are Eli's children, all Hophni and Phineases
Good Old Boys at the church barbecue ;
At home in this city where the offerings are made ;
Unmuzzled oxen, temporizing "perqs are few",
Picking up just a few choice cuts where-ever we may,
Fattening our priestly hearts on slaughter day.
We are mildly bothered by our inability
To chastise our children for their bolder excesses ;
Too well larded by all these steaks and chops,
To be able to deal with their fleshier messes.

Therefore, though we sit at the temple door
Or gather (as of old) at the city gate ;
It isn't to minister to the poor and lame
Or confront any enemy or evil we hate.
We gather just to eat and talk -- to talk while we eat.
We're fat cats like Eli, teetering on his seat.

James Howard Trott

A MOUSEHOLE SABLE

Locusts launched by density
Feed in flocks and blindly flee :
An image lovely to despise
We muse -- who nourish private lives.

Independence is our excuse to rebel
Not only against those who would compel,
But against all sorts of interdependence --
Common hopes, goals, wealth or attendance.

None shall make locust meals our fare !
This our pledge. What banner to bear ?
What high heraldry shall mark our divorsal --
A mousehole sable and a moldy morsel.

ON SEPARATION OF CHURCH AND STATE

Two children were killed, five were injured
Beneath the fall of a wind-whipped flagpole,
Long rod bringing harsh discipline
On contending St. Barnabus' school ground.
Immediately the church sent out inspectors
To see to the security of staffs elsewhere ;
Perhaps to ask what flag the catholic should fly,
To whom the church owes fealty.
The blow those children were not spared
(Always the innocent for our sins)
Was struck at the butt of a hand-hewn idol

2.

Which cannot stand in the winds of adversity.
Who knows better than St. Barnabus,
Comes a time for separation.

RUSTED OUT BURNING BARRELS

The glowing ashes in the rusted out burning barrels
Along the dirt-road alleys we walked home from school
Were oracles spoke clearly of mortality
Which message we embraced, without question,
Because they-it were friends all our short lives.
Sweet-sour the smell of burning garbage.)
Perhaps the sight and smell of kitchen and yard waste
Did not offend anyone then because of recent experience
(Yes, current for many) of dealing with more noisome
Waste and odors. Most farms still had privies,
And therefore most of us had few illusions about
The fundamental tidiness of human endeavor.
Now the town has progressed and ordinances require
New barrels, tight lids, and no burning.
Mortality is dead. Decay has been banished.
In our childish days it was obscene
To take down your pants in public,
But death could be mentioned and even faced --
Mrs. Heunig, the venerable next-door neighbor
Who held me to the window so I might wave to Mother
And see my own house from another's perspective,
Died in that small clapboard home, ancient and honorable.
Mortality the idea, but death the fact: an acquaintance.

There is a retirement home now, so that the aged
May (must?) fade from every day into no day,
Very hygenically like the refuse and wastes.
Babies grew inside mothers in those times --
From little tiny things to kicking dynamos of life
Inside their homes of flesh and it was a common privilege
To be allowed to feel them kick. Now, however,
There are no babies, only fetuses -- until bang of birth
When depending on tests, economics and parental mood,
They may be transformed into human beings.
Beginnings are no more, and ends increasingly obscure
Unless there is some lingering glow in this world
Like a rusted out burning barrel.

REACH ME

Reach me, Oh Lord,
Behind the drawn down shades of my mountains ;
In dreary depths of my sighing seas ;
As far as earnest east from wistful west --
Reach thou me.

Reach me, Oh Lord,
Floating amidst corpuscular moments of time ;
Wandering labyrinthine tunnelled thought ;
Wracked and fluttering far-flung by winds of passion --
Reach thou me.

Reach me, Oh Lord,
Worm away the gourd that succours me from thee ;
Tornado my tabernacles, consume by Baal-built altars,
Lead me into alien spaces where your light unhindered
May shine upon my startled head -- there reach me,
Oh, Lord -- cause me to reach toward thee.

II. THE INFAMY

DEMANDS, DESIRES, WANTS, NEEDS

Demands, desires, wants, needs :
These the grist for human greed,
These the teeth in the gaping maw
That snaps at God and tears the law.

Demands, desires, wants, needs :
The crowds' cry, the mobs' creed ;
List compiled by men and a snake
Crawling through this thorny brake.

Demands, desires, wants, needs :
There was one, though guaranteed
All of these and eternally more,
Who, abandoning all, opened Heaven's door.

(First published in *Cornerstone* Magazine, 1983)

MODERN MAN

Modern man -- evolution's peak :
One hand in the stars, while the other parts
Limb from limb -- a sideshow geek
With space agued mind and stone aged heart.

ADEQUATE COVERAGE

In case of catastrophe . . .
. . . Like a thief in the night
To provide for the future . . .
. . . Walk by faith not by sight
Some measure of comfort . . .
. . . She gave her last cent . . .
Who cares not for his own . . .
. . . Having these be content . . .
Use wisely the mammon of unrighteousness . . .
. . . Sell all and follow me . . .
We must be good stewards . . .
. . . Tonight 'tis required of thee.

IN THE DEATH CAMP

The most mind-whalloping facts of our bare age
Come out of news and recent history.
Scepticism is allowed in matters of spirit,
Or in many things feeling of emotion,
But all are true believers in Buchenwald,
Auschwitz and Bergen-Belsen.
For this reason Solzhenitsyn caught us off guard
With accounts of a Gulag just as starkly awful,
And started us on a fearful thought-path :
Once is the exception that proves the rule ;
Twice is co-incidence, but a third time . . .
Would mean a pattern.
Since nearly two million unborn infants per year
Is not sufficient to persuade the scientific,
I leave that horror for others to ignore ;
But return to a fact none living disputes,
That we all are ash-bound in a death camp.

In the camps, most accounts agree,
There were many sorts of soul and conduct :
Men, women, children accepting their lot
With various kinds of adaptation.
Some despaired, and if not immediately murdered,
Died of no longer wishing to live.
Some struggled on, clinging to skeletons
Of what must have seemed ancient, alien ethics :
Giving charity where they could, seeking justice
In the narrow scope of the greater infamy.

But some (would it be too much to say many?)
Became what we call (without elegance) "survivors",
Not necessarily those who lived through,
But those who lived as if nothing else mattered :

Picking up where we have never left off,
With a kind of bare-bones capitalism :
The sort of thing that makes Ayn Rand ridiculous --
Greater good of caring for none but oneself.

And so as the herds were branded and culled
And prepared for the slaughter, too many grazed
Intent on their fattening, growing suet for soap
To wash the butts of their satanic butchers.

It is very much like that in our death camp,
Except for the intolerable star-minded few
Who lay down their lives for their friends.

THE CREED/THE HERETIC

(antiphonal) Molecular in generation, worship one
       Through aeonic forms and stages now become
  (unison)   Highest creature on the earth,
       Though mayhem mark his life and birth,
       A holy son.

(a.)   From a gram of ninety-second comes a flash :
   Energy from matter rages, fire from ash.
(u.)   Miracle to preach to nations,
       Threatening death bright revelation -
       Adam smashed.

(a.)   Truth subsists in matters proven, *cogito ergo sum*
            All there is we'll one day know, let that day come.
(u.)   Trust your mind and trust no others,
              Data banks are our true brothers,
              Hymns they hum.

(a.)   Urges rule us in all matters, live and eat
            Biological our motives, glands secrete.
(u.)   Though we practice sublimation
              All mankind of every nation
              Is in heat.

(a.)   Empty gods and spirits taunt us on our beds.
            Outworn myths these are that haunt us, skins to shed.
(u.)   Man is matter, life is motion,
              Spirit is a bygone notion,
              Kill it dead.

(a.)   Every man is but a product, mutants few,
            Bits of endless generations, sum in you.
(u.)   Common the equations of us all [interupted - a
cry]

    (Heretic)   Yet I unbalanced tip the scales and fall
                At heaven's feet; there say my creed a-dieu!

(earlier version pub'd in New Life News, church newsletter of New Life
Church Jenkintown, PA with note:"copyright James H. Trott September
1983")

III. COUNTING THE COST

GOOD

The doing of good may motivate all
Brief beings, do-gooders below heaven.
Purpose is a pliant plant
With roots extending through all time,
Meeting, opposing, strangling others.

The fretting suicide, philanthropically
Thinks to unburden friends and family.
Satan, also, some still believe,
Humanely offered good to Eve.
Sought Judas good, a world cure
As world utopia's provocateur ?
The fleeing husband's heart-halving love :
May it be good, evil spoken of ?
Unless one numbers every jot and tittle,
Our few meaner acts signify little
Beside bolder prints of noble plans :
Unceasing efforts to do good to man.
Goods in boxes, gods carved of wood
Are all made, sold, for mankind's good.

Ah, what is good? Is evil good ?
Must anything stand to say "it stood"?
Yet one treated titular good as fraud,
Declared to man none good but God.
That not-so-good meddler, wild fanatic,
Despoiler of all goods, Hebrew and Attic,
Imposed himself without reason or rhyme,
Ignoring men's goods, obligations, time :
Imperiously un-good, worse than suicide, jilter,

Tumbled man's good around him a-kilter . . .
And lunatic, drove all creation to groan,
Abandoning all good -- even his own.

SELF-IMMOLATION

Molech it was, if I remember, demanded first-born fuel.
His embers glowed; yet none served him, faithful fool
So wasteful as to burn himself, self-immolant.
It is a modern stimulant to read of Marxist martyrs,
Dedicated blower-aparters of selves with enemies; Vietnam
Buddhists' stand for peace shrilled fiery acts
Into all ears. With fatal facts, monks made impacts.
Muslims, Buddhists, no doubt a Hindu or two. What of you
Christian few? Touched by the flaming torch you carry ?

Fire-blinded Paul's mention of marrying, burning,
We learn early and at first hint of heat
We meet, we drop the question of singularity,
Conclude a parity between what is and what ought
Remain the piteous lot of whom hot cupid never shot.

If but those self-cindered masses over there (soon here?)
Held dear God-given life worth half as much (not more)
Instead of adoring Nothing, which is nothing at last,
And refused to be cast into water and into fire,
Their pyres themselves lighting (the thought be abhorred.)
Let us then pour it, the volatile fuel of faith
And lay the match (remaining unmarried if we may or must)

To thrust back-fires, counter flames against the holocaust
These lost engulfs, the world's souls withering
Who blind are slithering toward everlasting flame ;
Cry out the name of the Self-Immolant, hell-melting,
Whose light, heat, welding men to God, and to each other
Turning us, our Brother, weds us to the burning.

IV. BATTLE AT THE GATES

WHERE ARE THE GATES ?

The faithful have abandoned what they once occupied ;
Spun, turning to the world the un-armed side ;
Retreated before a banner bearing "Scientific truth".
Agreeing a stand impossible, lacking the weapon "proof".
Thus the church ran a distance, then built a redoubt ;
Barricaded behind steel doors that only swung out --
Beneath banners "religion" and "belief" and "spirit" ;
Abandoning the phenomenal sphere -- beginning to fear it.
Some reluctant to retreat were left behind, it's true :
Artists and intellectuals, some blithe-minded few, who,
Either made pax by so adjusting their allegiance
That only their old uniforms lent any air of credence,
Or those mocked and surrounded until they were hid
From all, though valiantly stood and valourously did.
Back in the new headquarters (a kind of upper room),
The faithful boasted to dispel the latent gloom,

By claiming it worthless: the field doomed to burn,
And congratulating one another on knowing when to turn.

Until (a divisive deed) someone read the orders,
Given ages earlier in defense of the kingdom's borders.
Lo! The command was clear, the injunction not to fail ;
A prophecy the Enemy's gates never might prevail.
A hearty strategist or two called the others cattle
For promoting the silly myth that gates go to battle,
Instead of the clear bugle call old soldiers knew well :
Heaven sends its offense to the very doors of hell,
Where those which did not prevail to hold the General out,
Shall give before the church and fall with a shout.

Why so many yet in hiding in or under bed,
Withdrawn still from hell's gates in unbelief and dread?

JUDAS LOVED

Judas loved someone -- too much some would say.
Loved with a consuming love, loved I pray
Less than you or I love, less or more :
Love thirty pieces worth or to a dying-for.

Love is a word, like Judas' love, a word that shrinks
Or swells, fades or glows more than a Judas thinks --
Word without concrete type; not yet (for Judas never) ;
A word that can excuse a lot, though not forever.

We kill the things we say we love, like poor Judas,
Because the heart and acts of love still elude us ;
Because we love ourselves, which is no love either,
Or if we must hurt with joy we'd rather have neither.

Judas' love turned about a world of Judas' making,
A world of Judas' planning, of his earth-shaking.
He could not, would not love One to it a stranger :
So afraid he'd lose his world, he saw no other danger.

Judas hoped against hope (loved against love),
That Jesus would throw down Rome (angels from above).
Judas hoped his killing Christ would make Christ live.
So false lovers still have nought but death to give.

(Accepted by **Cornerstone** Magazine, 1992)

V.   THE LITTLEST BROTHERS

INFANT MORTALITY

I went to quintessential college
Full of the sense of my own potential,
Robust with the prospect of things to come,
Full of fervor for my own importance.
Not long after I hopped the continent
And landed in a place of brick and dust,
I sought respite, a freshening of my zeal
With kindred in a greener town.

Little did I know before -- nothing --
Until my uncle opened eternity's broad door :
Telling me my mother miscarried there,
A thing I only dimly dredged
From images of a childhood mystery.
My brother, my sister, I know not,
Passed into the limitless unseen
Without so much as greeting me.
Returning to Cambridge I heard
Pompery but peep, saw circumstance cower,
And my own importance run off into the distance.

PEOPLE WHO ARE STARED AT

I see you blinking for a bus,
People who are stared at,
Today and many yesterdays.
I ask you if you can forgive
My burning coals of glances.
Distinctive still, you haunt me
From far off schoolroom smells
And rattling of restaurants ;
Your eyes or lip or limbs, your shape,
Not Hollywood's, not eugenics',
Are not your only hallmarks.
For you have learned that shuffling look,
The posture of confused shame,

Embarrassment without fault.
On a vacation, was I nine ?
Stopping at a roadside inn,
We found no table of a size for all,
So normal Pete and I both sat
On round, perfect lunchbar stools
Next to a man one stared at.
Knowing then, first time? the wrong,
I kept on glancing, stared at him
Until self-consciousness had choked
Stopped his throat, his mouth mid-meal.
Quickly, awkward, up he rose
To pay his bill and hurry out --
Out of this place of god-damned kids
With healthy, normal, staring eyes.
Forgive me, brother, please forgive,
People who are stared at.

TATTERNALIA

The schoolyard is empty on this rare raw day
Empty not just partly as when the children play
Before or after or at times in between
Regimented hours of learning . . . things don't mean . . .

Things don't mean because there's no firm order here;
None but chance arrangements, notes of random reporter
Of fully independent means and independent employment
Who sees no time sacred in this girl or boy spent . . .

Girl or boy spent time is recorded by their spending :
Here see the wind gather mail of their sending :
Red and orange, white and blue wraps of old rations,
Dancing a circle little girl and boy fashion . . .

Little girl and boy fashion tatters whirl around
As though in a dance, making hardly a sound
But the tolling of a rolling can at the rear,
Not catching the rest, but hurrying for fear . . .

Hurrying for fear this reckless dance abruptly ends,
For fear an end already come: that the dance portends
Done: boys and girls made tatters, torn from wraps
In greedy haste, sacrificed in fear for scraps . . .

Scraps in a ring: plastic, paper, a can behind,
Brings not living children, but dead to mind --
Dead discards in a corner of playground wider,
Like carcases of flies in the orb of some spider . . .

The orb of some spider -- my orb, my eye,
Sees the whirlwind bodies in the blown-by bits
Of a mad and empty dance. We have sucked life away:
The saturnalia generation -- have preyed. -- Now pray.

CAUGHT RED-HANDED

Since Cain, blood has been the sign :
Blood the indisputable witness, calling out
From the grounds of death, "guilty, guil--ty!"
An endless flow of thorn-bled trickles cannot answer,
Cannot atone, nor blood of bulls and animals,
Though those signs, too, were testimony.
Nor does kosher cleanness keep man from death --
Every hand looks like Lady MacBeth's
If only as a result of folding,
Of saying nothing, not rising in warning
Though carefully washed like Pilate's in the morning.
Thus the expression is applied full breadth
To cookie-thieving, to delivering death,
And all hands, be they handy or sleek
Are caught red-handed. No blood speaks
Better unless better blood be found
Poured from clean hands on this sin-stained ground.

TERMINATION

Termination, a term of endearment :
Good fences make good neighbors ;
Endings make beginnings; life feeds on death.
And so it is the most detached, the most clinical,
Most professional (professing what?)
Word for murder -- grimly ironical
In books about the Mafia or Gestapo ;
But medically proper from the abortionist.

18.

To terminate sounds like an ending --
And certainly is -- for someone ;
But also the start of some things interminable.

VI. OPPRESSED ACCESSORIES

FROM AUSPICES TO AUGURS

From auspex to augur the seer has devolved :
Diving from heaven's to earth's bodies' bowels :
Like a fallen angel resolved to become a mite,
A bacterium: this his spiteful joy.
So now our pioneers of right cure souls
By killing the girl or boy within
And call demurring sin. Once the holy
Studied signs in heaven, watched creatures fly
And clouds and stars dance to mystical songs.
Now the priest gropes in the shoally places
Of a woman's organs, chants "die" as his knife
Traces magic death for her who longs to know
Death as life, rejoices to mourn, and would
Divine destiny in her dissected unborn.

A WOMAN'S BODY -- THE SCENE OF THE CRIME
1 . SHE

Among her transgressions deserving death
One, at least , won't be charged against her --
She did not leave the scene of the crime (alive).
The clues were clear: blood type, fingerprints,
And all her body parts were accounted for --
Except for her face which the assailant obliterated.
(Is one absent, not a person, without a face?
If one has no face may one be a victim?)
But there was no doubt about who she was,
Even apart from genetic evidence ("science").
A name was written on the body bag: her mother's,
The woman who was the scene of the crime.

2. HE

Another crime against society as we know it
Was perpetrated by this driven individual
Upon a woman's body.
More astonishing, to many more horrifying,
Than all the other crimes around us,
The murders, the rapes, the various ravages
Committed against and upon the weaker sex
(Not even cult leaders concoct theologies
Of equitable vengeance against Eve
To defend these offenses).
First he spoke suggestively to her,
Received her untutored assent, then
When she (near-child) was unconscious,
He entered in, made a baby,
To experience pain, where pain had never been.
Although the child seemed at first normal,
It was not long before her heart was broken,

As He continued on his father's perverse course.
After his execution, friends asked for the remains.
They let her bury what was left of him,
Gave the woman his body, the scene of the crime

APPALACHIA IN SUBURBIA

We ain't never had nothin', don't know what it means
To own a home, be happy on our own piece of land.
The old man scrapes by, night ridge-runnin' man,
Drunk most the time on sixty-hour dreams

Of makin' it, while the kids grown wild :
Barefoot-souled and hungry for executive love
That I can't give 'em, don't have enough of
To even mean "precious" to my littlest child.

Ya, we got the big mortgaged split-level shack.
Sure, three cars and a place at the shore,
But you're hungry if you have to have more,
You're always dirt-poor when you live out lack.

In her pinch-cheeked, hollow, self-starved eyes,
In the grim-faced smoothness of her moonshine man,
There is poverty deep as a dream that lies:
Appalachia surrounds us -- give if you can.

JUSTICE

I killed you
Now you're killing me,
I guess it's justice
Just as poetry
Never bends
But rhyme at the end.

I thought it was an operation
Removing a growth,
A growth on me, a soul-sapping part
But no parasite devours
Anyone's body
As your death consumes my heart.

If I had lost you after birth
Or killed you in a passion --
Experienced or caused your loss
In any other fashion,
I would repent, I would regret
Less and more than I have yet.

That is the justice,
They said "fine", that you were mine
To dispense with before breath.
Now all my days belong to you.
Nothing I do, but through and through,
Is tinged and weighted by your death.

Jesus trade this justice for mercy !
Baby we killed be born in me !

VII. TREMOR IN GETHSEMANE

THE CENTURIONS

We the dead salute you. So they say centurions said
An admirable vow, though morbid. Indeed we all are dead
Before long, and why not join mortality to some scheme :
An empire, a cause, a fraternal effort or dream.
But if Caesar dreams a roaring pyre fueled with the wood
Of soldier limbs, soldier vows and fool-hardihood --
As often he did: if Caesar be Gengis Khan, Nero, or Stalin,
Is blind loyalty admirable among the files or the fallen?

It is said there was no captive of faith in all Israel,
Like that centurion who carried his mantle so well,
Knowing how to obey orders and how to issue commands --
Under authority, yet with power in his hands
To send, enforce, call back -- seeing with other eyes.
Which earned him deathbound praise, a backward Caesar's
          prize.
Rome could not hold his allegiance against one higher.
He submitted to a leader pledged to perish on a pyre.

Not as diplomatic perhaps as Capernaum's soldier saint,
Peter claimed his perogative, a higher law's restraint,
And said, Whether better to obey man or God, you must
          decide,
But as for us we'll obey God, for which salute some died.
Two armies, then, we may descry, centurions heading each :
One bows before "the law", in no case brooks its breach ;
The other saluting one dead who lives, sure of no law but his.
Lest we think this impractical, we should remember this :

At Nuremburg soldier files saluted another Reich,
Testifying to absolute faith in a Caesar not unlike
Old Rome's, saying "we obeyed our legal orders,"
Raising consternation among both judges and warders,

Who, though relativists, like so many in judgment's hall,
Could not excuse the enormity of the infamy withal.
Indited under some higher law, those brought before the bar,
Were saluted with death for obeying a law but of their Czar.

OUR DEBT TO HUMANITY

Must be paid.
What's the bill, the bottom line :
Thirty pieces or a talent hid,
The widow's mite or the highest bid ?

ASH WEDNESDAY AT DUSK

Ashes to ashes, dust to dusk,
Our days pass away like our flesh.
Tonight the dying forehead of day
Is streaked with cloudy wisps of ash.
I come from a brief stay in a cell
And yet the sky itself is barred

With purple and blue –
No escaping this prison.
There is suffering and death
Yet to see, to bear, to be locked in
This cell of flesh
We have been lent
To pass this hastening Lenten time.

See the message scrawled by another prisoner?

VIII. PILATE THE POLITICIAN

LIFE, LIBERTY, AND THE PURSUIT OF HAPPINESS

Life, liberty, and the pursuit of happiness
Knit together in a nation's womb.

Life, liberty, and their happy pursuit
Grew and flourished as God-given fruit.

Happiness, liberty, and precious life
Are now cut apart by the doctor's knife.

The nation might, unlike the baby,
Through faith and repentance revive -- maybe

TRUTH OR TRUTHS?

Art thou king of the Jews
Pilate asked one accused
By a people unused
To the saying of sooths :
Such difficult clues
As this prophet used.

Yet with so much to lose
The madman refused
To make an excuse,
Or grasp Roman thews :
To claim mercy his dues,
As the sane man sues ;

Rather waxed so enthused
As to ask Pilate's views --
'Your question is whose?
I'm not one who brews
Wars, nor world kingdom woos.
Truth alone is my news.'

Then Pilate, confused ;
No longer amused ;
Sick-hearted; perused
The prisoner obtuse.
Said, 'let the crowd choose . . .
Say not truth but truths.'

CONVICTED or PIN THE TAIL ON THE DONKEY

Would the donkey were as this justice blind,
Who would on him these sharp tales pin,
But his path by a standing angel was blocked,
Strange royal fairies put a spell on him,
And he cannot now but halt and speak,
Though Hosanna be Crucify inside a week.

Blindness among self-styled seers is vice --
These who pierce the side of the speaking dumb
With legal points, append a proper tally ;
Who bring justice to all by injustice on some.
But this spell of love they cannot lift,
The donkey's head turns their sentence a gift.

The conviction took place, the tail was pinned
Before these games -- the tale was wound up.
Once prophet for profit or running away
Now impeded, impelled, his fate bound up,
Though often he asks for another saddle
Or longs to graze with the thousand cattle.

This judge pins a sentence above his head,
Which belongs behind him; followed after
The lasting conviction which upon him rides,
Who saw the angel and heard fairy laughter.
They label him ass, though he prophesy
Bear a child away, lumber back to die.

He's a donkey's colt, his tale small,
In a train of beasts, fools for slaughter.
He's but one among wavering wood-bound weavers
Beloved by heaven, son or daughter.

He bears another with his tale in his hands :
The Judge who his own blood demands.

DEODAND

*A personal chattel which was the immediate cause of the death of a
rational creature, and for that reason given to God, that is,
forfeited to the crown, to be applied to pious uses, and distributed
in alms by the high almoner. Thus if a cart ran over a man and
killed him, it was forfeited as a deodand.* -- Blackstone

"Given to God", a phrase from days and a far place
Before men's law was divorced from the grace
Of the high almoner -- now with no legal trace.

Destruction of rational beings is not strange,
Things stay the same the more they change,
But the concept of chattel has been rearranged.

Now by no accident, but by custom and "right",
We snuff out lives which have not seen the light
Of day nor tossed an hour in this world's night.

Which is the deodand by that ancient doom --
The scalpel? the saline? the hand? or the womb
The unborn is torn from? or the fatal room ?

Or perhaps the truck that dumps the remains
With the waste of a nation which nothing restrains
But deadly disease and capital gains ?

Might products made from this un-named be named
Deodand, giving goddess-like beauty as claimed
So that none anointed ever need look ashamed?

Or is the "birth matter", this strange organ "foetus"
Itself the chattel, as of old slaughtered meat was
Offered to gods whose priests cried "feed us".

Perhaps there's no point in disagreeing
Over old legal terms of foreign decreeing
Concerning an unseen, unwanted being.

Here the doctor and woman conspire in fraud --
Claim the cause, thus forfeit (by old law abroad)
Is the child, at its own death "given to God".

IX. VISITATIONS OF PRISONERS

LINES IN JAIL

Where but in this place
Might I digest the grace
You have heaped upon my plate ;
Locked up in me, its unjust fate.

How else might you contain such awe
And awesome glory beyond the law :
Shekinah-powered pulses that betray
And break upon this jail of clay.

For grace too free may be worse
Than (best for Adam's race) the curse ;
And as rhyme and meter help make verse
Poetry, here grace I best rehearse.

Bound tightly before willing to be bound,
Once free and lost -- now prisoner found.

CRICKETS AT KEY ROAD

In an orderly world where silence is cleanliness
The stridulations of the crickets are an offense ;
The well-provided birds never obey lawful orders.

PHONE CALL

Ten minutes during which clouds begin to part,
The sun stands still and there is unity --
The dividing wall is broken down,
The body is one
Through words and brief-built plans,
Snatches of information,
Paragraphic portrayals of affection,
And the guard says, "Time's up.

"Every relief is a promise, a pledge as well as a passing meal."
- George MacDonald

THE VISIT

Who are these people not wearing green?
The room belongs to the prison --
It is guarded and watched,
Yet here they are, people I have seen,
It seems a dream.

And they take my hand,
They embrace me,
Speak words of courage.
Are they my own race,

Free to come and go?
They tell me so,
And promise love and a hope
That I have deliberately
Left out of my calculations.

They ask me and I talk
Far too much, for time cataracts
Away though I want them to say
So much more.
But another voice says "time's up".

And when I leave I must submit
To stripping and being searched
For contraband, dangerous substances or tools
They might have passed me.
FOOLS! They gave me love!

CHRIST IS MY PRISON

Though creation have no bounding wall,
Christ is my prison, my cell, my all.
The works he has prepared are my yard,
The Paraclete is cellmate and guard.

WAKE-UP

A volley of electric locks murders sleep,
Executes time's judgment.
Out damned spot -- and Rover and Tray,
Out for master Pavlov's offering :

We will rehabilitate you.
We will box the quick bamboo.
We will bind the erring feet
With fear for an shackle-shoe.

With fear of fines, confines and finitudes
Without mercy, without life, without flexibility.
Open your eyes to morning that has closed --
The king all but dead among his kinsmen.

'Tis only a ghost haunts our feast, bacchanal,
Our screeching and dancing around our kettle.
We have caught lizards' eyes, and adders' tongues,
All under control, soon the spell is done.

And if we cannot clearly predispose,
At least their lives we traumatize --
For when they hate, they worship us :
Gnashing our name engraves it in stone.

Yet -- the spotted hand appears ever spotted . . .
And the unlocked hearts we cannot capture.

STAY IN YOUR CELL

If you stay in your cell
No one will ever get you --
No one can touch or hurt you
Or frighten you by force
(Except the supernumery
Guardians of good or ill).
But if you leave your cell,
Who knows what awful freedom
You may find . . . or give others.

If He had stayed in his cell . . .

POSTING BOND

The only picture in the files was Caesar's.
They took, his prints, his hands
And covered thern with red ink.
Someone official (bureaucracies are always obscure)
Asked where he came from,
His address and social security number.

Unable to find the proper file,
Hands washed eachother,
Popular politics were carefully considered,
And overcrowding in the jails relieved.

They denied his bail,
Though he paid the bond :
Took the rap for his homeboys
As well as his bondsmen.

X.   NINEVAH'S DOOM -- OR SODOM'S?

ARRESTIVE

The only religious crime in old pragmatic Rome
Was to fail to adore the emperor in minor sacrifice.
Though few believed a god in him dwelt at home,
All agreed to mouth the creed was civilized and nice.

The only religious crime in pragmatic America
Is to hallow and defend defenseless human lives --
Believe God's image linked to the placenta --
Hinder hired unholy knives.

The ancient church was arrested nor treated lightly :
Lions ate unbowed limbs, human flares blazed nightly ;
But now the church rests, grown prematurely festive.
Unbow! None arrests these crimes if none grows restive.

(Growing restive is defined as getting restless from having rested too
long.)

BURIED AT THE CROSSROADS

In ancient days bodies of condemned and hanged men
Were buried not in churchyards but where main roads
      crossed:
No holy ground for stony hearts beyond redeeming --
No peace attended lost bones, traffic streaming.
Thus one condemned of crime in time further remote
Was executed on a cross-tree far outside the camp;
All dignity, respect and honor made a joke
On him: they smote him, watched him cramp, and lastly
      choke.

If you and I will not submit to this world's rules of play,
No holy ground will be reserved for our cold memory's
      bones.
Who names as home the center of the cross is sowed
Where meet the ways; yet sown, will soar at time's crossroad.

BIBLICAL GEOGRAPHY

Tarshish is only a whale's length from Ninevah.

WOMB AND TOMB

Every womb opens on the grave.
No Lazarus comes forth for long
From that tomb cave.
All go back
To mother earth by father death,
Seed harvested in exhaustion
Borne off on exhaled breath,
Sower's songs to labor's cries.
Birth is death's twin ;
Parturition, parting,
Meet again, one taking
What the other brought.
Hurts renewed, dim fears remembered,
Too, go shortly to their dooms.
Can any light extinguish dark
In these stone-sealed rooms ?
Unless enduring father force them
Graves will not be wombs.

THE STARLINGS

Congregate on bare bone trees
Finding them lovely with the sound of their peeping,
Fly in flocks, flitter and flutter ;
Always become silent 'til they alight somewhere,
Following the croak of the moment's leader;
Then instant proceed to proclaim and shout,
Catching from each other what to carry on about --
A while.   Winter comes

THE LIONS

My soul is among lions . . . Psalm 57

Darius himself was torn in enforcement of his law
Which condemned Daniel to die among the beasts,
Just and merciful ruler caught between lions :
One prowling about seeking whom he might devour,
The other fierce offspring of Judah.

Nero of later empire empathized less with those
Lamb-led exiles laid down with his lions.
He threw himself willing between devourer's jaws
Long before loosing colosseum cats.

Some kneeling in paw-printed dust
May have hoped for Daniel's reprieve,
Prey to the brief error,
Praying for another's deliverance.

Darius came early to the stone-sealed den,
After fasting the slow night in doubt, fear.
Fasted too those lions, though late of Babylonia.
Man-fed Romans fasted never, gorging their maws
On those who hoped
Life began in their long entrails.

The lion shadow among those lambs
Driving them to merciless slaughter
Was far fiercer than the mangy prowler without,
As Darius' law of Medes and Persians
Was lenient beside Daniel's God's ;
As Darius' mercy was harsh beside that emperor's
Who himself condemned, himself consumed,
Nor shut his lion's mouth,

Who lifted up his tattered carcass --
Food for the lion-torn.

SECTION TWO : PRO-LIFE POEMS (1967-1988)

BOBBY

The tent itself appeared uninhabitable,
Constricted, awry, grotesque.
When he moved in, so he told a friend,
The repairman said it couldn't last.
Seventy-two years it lasted, long enough.

But out of that tent, stretched and contorted,
Came the most wonderful signs --
Supernatural unsung songs,
And barely comprehensible glorious rejoicings.
None could pass by without marvelling
At the contrast of house and householder.

Yet all he had was that slack-sinewed space
Mysteriously knit by one tentmaker
Who hems in all he loves,
And for those who love him --
Works all threads together for good.

The tent was a gift to Bobby,
Bobby a gift to us,
That we might learn to long for more fitting
Bodies, and dwellings, and home.

(First published in *New Horizons*, April, 1985)

41.

"C"- SECTION

They were professionals
Who fastened you cruciform,
Hardboiled wisemen
With their radio playing,
Yet what their hands did
Was so far out of their hands
They might as well have admitted it,
For the Father picked you out
While the world was in utero
To suffer that I might have life:
To come to the point
Where you needed him desperately
To help me know I did, too.
When that blade sliced your abdomen,
Blood mingled with water
And I knew there was a curse.
When that life came forth,
I knew the curse was lifted.

NO WONDER

The men whose wives,
Yea, mothers, too, whose daughters
Are but afterbirths to their desires,
Ought not to rock in such surprise
When daughters treat their own likewise --
Destroying the afterbirths of their desires
As tissue without life-value.

It takes some fortitude, a particular vision
Alien to man and woman-kind
To affirm and cherish ones womb's fruit
When you yourself are destitute.

PEOPLE WHO ARE STARED AT

I see you blinking for a bus,
People who are stared at,
Today and many yesterdays.
I ask you if you can forgive
My burning coals of glances.
Distinctive still, you haunt me
From far off schoolroom smells
And rattling of restaurants;
Your eyes or lip or limbs, your shape,
Not Hollywood's, not eugenics',
Are not your only hallmarks.
For you have learned that shuffling look,
The posture of confused shame,
Embarrassment without fault.
On a vacation, was I nine?
Stopping at a roadside inn,
We found no table of a size for all,
So normal Pete and I both sat
On round, perfect lunchbar stools
Next to a man one stared at.
Knowing then, first time? the wrong,
I kept on glancing, stared at him

Until self-consciousness had choked,
Stopped his throat, his mouth mid-meal.
Quickly, awkward, up he rose
To pay his bill and hurry out --
Out of this place of god-damned kids
With healthy, normal, staring eyes.
Forgive me, brother, please forgive,
People who are stared at.

THIS LITTLE LIGHT OF MINE

I cannot show it here
Nor spend it on now's moment.
It's saved for when the hour is reached
Where ambiguity is breached
. . .For when I'm sure.

I once was told I carried it
Upon my person heaven-sent,
Then cautioned I should use it well
To light my path away from hell
. . .If I could keep it lit.

But I have yet to find a place
Wherein I dared to burn it bright.
Those yet have been so very dark,
And I have known no certain mark
. . .Sure spark in any face.

Some day my flame will shine
When there is no more night.
Or must I take the awful chance
And in the darkness make it dance
. . .This little light of mine?

(First published in *Cornerstone*, summer 1984)

WEAPONRY

Some people's lives are canister,
Some people's cannon ball.
Some people's lives are rifle fire,
Some people's misfires all.
Some people must muzzle load,
Some fire like automatics,
Some launch long range missiles,
Others hurl sharp sticks.
Comparisons of range and power,
Their contrasting ballistics
May sometimes be of interest
To students armed with statistics;
But after the shooting stops,
The question will be framed,
Not how loaded, how big, how loud,
But which way each was aimed.

(First published in *The Banner*, Grand Rapids.)

SESSALG DERORRIM NI NAM EHT

The man in mirrored glasses walked demented,
Hidden in the noon-day sun.
Twin lenses flashed a code,
Some ancient obscure heliography.

Beneath the looking glasses
Snowwhite teeth froze a smile, fading not,
Prophetic glory reflecting
Blinding in-sight.

I looked the striding in the face
But for a moment, saw myself there
In glass, under glass, friends and nation
Reflected darkly.

What secret malice preened
Itself behind lenses
Through which one might see
Others seeing but oneself?

In twin mirrors facing one another
One may see both, myriad,
In a moment diminish.
Infinity flashes each to each.

We stand before single spectacles
To balm pride, hair, or body,
To review times's passages,
But these lenses faced none, themselves.

Bright lenses facing outward told no tale,
Hinted not yet cried some great

Emptiness behind, blackened mirrorback,
Pitch or paint; backward eyes if any.

When men in mirrored glasses meet
In flashing dual reciprocation,
There in tense reflections
Who can bare their eyes to see?

MAN EMBARRASSED

I saw a man embarrassed
By the age of the woman on his arm,
(His mother, grandmother, mother-in-law?)
He hurried toward the nursing home doors,
In order to be relieved of her.

A man embarrassed
By age on his arm
Hurried toward the home
To be relieved of her.

Man embarrassed by age,
Hurried home
To be relieved.

Man, embarrassed,age,
Hurry, relieved.

Embarrassed?

DARK SHADOW

A dark shadow, small and mean
Towers the years beyond each child
In the shadowbox of imagination,
Fills waking dreams with vague dreads.
Yet the eye, nor the mind's eye,
Sees time, neither lame nor halt,
Run fears backward,
As childish shadows grow and yet
Are swallowed by the foraging light.
Radiant, bright and taller than Babel,
The unseeable cross pulls shadows in --
See the living child of God
Light from each child the shades of sin.

EPITAPH

He died I fear as did his nation
From great excess of moderation.

DOMINOES

Dominoes that face each other
Fall together, sister, brother.
But out of step, one stops the fall,
Rescues those after, one and all.

GIVING OUR CHILDREN WHAT WE NEVER HAD

I don't want my children to know poverty like I did --
I don't want them to feel the lack
Which rode so much upon my boy-man back.

We have worked hard to give our children
All the things we never had.

I want my children to be free to enjoy
The good things in life.

Sixty hours a week at the office,
Drinks and TV to unwind -- and parties,
Golf on weekends (you'd be surprised how many deals
Are wrapped up on the golf course).
The therapist has been good for both of us,
But she says she wants a quiet divorce.

We've been so busy giving our children
The things we didn't have
That we didn't ever get around
To giving them what we did.

THE LAST WORD

"Death be not!"
The love-torn dirge sounds deep and loud,
"Or if thou canst but be, then,
Death do not be proud."

"Do not go!"
The child pleads at the closing of the fight,
"Or if you go -- do not go gentle --
Into that (good?) night!"

"Grave, thy victory! Death, thy sting!"
Exclaim the anguished pair,
But out of hell itself replies
The last word -- "Where?"

IDOL-MAKING MACHINE

"Our hearts are idol-making machines" John Calvin

Hearts churn out their little gods.
Built for better, gone awry.
Heads make reasons, flesh sensations,
Hearts stamp idols, tool and die.

Idols are not evil stuff --
Wood for carving, wood for burning,
Gold for molding, gilding, shining.
Such were good were it enough.

But hearts are god assembly lines,
Turning good to God-blot bad.
Taking every gift, transforming,
Driving all creation mad.

Hearts are idol-minting presses,
Stamping out their worthless tin,
While our minds and voices hawk it,
Barkers 'midst the factory din.

If God does not foreclose, dismantle,
Forge anew, and scourge each clean,
All are bound to mindless pounding,
Making idols, made machines.

A CHILD BORNE

The heart of woman used to cry at reaching months end
'Another child not to be borne.'
Now Hippocrates' is hard and her own, resolved
'Another child not to be borne.'

A CHILD'S NATURAL DEATH

"Let the little children come to me..."

But Lord -- this haste!
These little ones that rush,
Lord -- the long years' waste!
Their guardian angels, Lord,
Are they so soon weary
That you must take their charges
Lives, barely begun in theory?
Jesus, we're not ready yet:
Had time barely enough to beget,
Grow to love, wonder what they'd be.
Lord, It cuts deep -- heart-deep. Do you see?
Say something, shed some light
Into this sorrow, our souls' dark night.
In this great loss what are we taught?

And he answers only "Forbid them not..."

Then, Lord, tear-blind, we let go,
In starkest faith, bare belief you know
What you're doing, taking back what you've given...

"Of such," he says, "are the kingdom of heaven."

SECTION THREE: OTHER PRO-LIFE POEMS 1989-2015

STREET PEOPLE

If we keep our eyes high our vision will be sated
With insurance towers, where once there were steeples.
We will see the comforting works of our hands,
Where dust never settles and no man stands.
But on the pavement, in alleys, or grated
Heating vents, crouch the small street peoples
Grown all-important, blotting out success,
Challenging the interests which wear a vest.
They deeply disturb our utopian minds
For we cannot explain them, they make no sense
To worshippers of gross national product
Or standards of living in pounds and pence.
They thumb their grubby noses nicely
And declare we've miscalculated precisely.

UNDERGOING PRIVATION

To be lonely one need not be Robinson Crusoed
Or be-calmed on plague-swept sea like the Mariner.
Americans, for instance, are lonely and think it normal.

Born out of surging independence, pride
In distance from the nearest friend, and fiestiness,
Our nation leads in the rhetoric of mutuality
And the furthest removes of isolation.

What is privacy but the state of deprivation?
What is independence but a self-sufficient lie?
Where are we going as people, as a nation,
Undergoing privation until we die?

THE WASTING OF OUR POWERS

The wasting of our powers consumes our hours,
Devours our days, incinerates our dust.
Our words tumble, are but the rumble
Of crumbling towers, counting cost in trust
Misplaced and dreams disgraced; traced in ink that fades,
While suns set; the proudest grow humble;
Memories forget and wander in parodies of charades;
Deaths laid hollow wastes where the worm worry cowers.

What powers had we? What hours sad we
Dropped through fingers, now that none lingers
To remind us of the loss. Tossed as spume and spray,
Every second, each day, each eon spent.
And all that we were lent, indeed every cent --
Whether million or ten -- shall be counted again.

DYING FOR GAIN

"For me to live is Christ and to die is gain"
Philippians 1:21

Both Apostle Paul and his modern sons
Are willing to be ground like milled grain:
The former investing in sky-high bonds;
The latter apparently dying for gain.

TALISMANIC

In the city of Talismania
Where people all worship stuff
They accumulate --
I presume they wait --
'Til The Day When We All Have Enough.

HEROD'S WELCOME

What is the proper etiquette
For greeting a newborn child?
Pharoah commanded the midwives
To send each back whence he came.
Though contemporary doctors and judges
Don't bother to find out his name,
Herod at least asked the wisemen
To find that out if they could --
And then threw a big welcome,
Rolling out the carpet of blood.

SHE KEPT HER BABY

She kept her baby
  --You mean instead of adoption
She chose to raise it,
  Took the motherhood option?
No, I mean she loved it
  And gave it life,
Rather than submit it
  To the bloody knife.

PAROLE (for Brigid)

On the night I was paroled, Daddy stayed in prison,
Locked behind cold federal bars for his kindly mission.
Jailed for others babies' lives, other dads forlorn,
Daddy couldn't pick me up, new-released, newborn.

Daddy stood, appealed to moms for stays of execution.
Stood again before a judge, skewed to prosecution --
Who though sworn on oath by God, worshipped legal
    letters,
Bound and criminal himself, put daddy into fetters.

I was freed from jail that night, (mommy did hard labor),
Daddy's sister stood beside her, (my life's with my
    neighbor).
Daddy, my conceiver, reached, had his arms around me,
Though he lay in distant cell -- in Christ felt and found me.

I would rather Daddy hugged me as he hugs me now,
But how much better are his hugs because he would not
    bow
To evil framed as justice to witness my parole --
He is a better daddy with Christ warden of his soul.

ARREST

I should not be here. I perform the duty of temple guards
Who refuse to do it -- who approach seldom and only
To arrest me. God I feel lonely! Hear me, father,
If the cup can pass.. whose feet lead through the grass?

It is Judas -- predicting betrayal hurt less than the fact:
Watching trust fail before me, I am passive to his kiss,
I know now I must walk the long road to do this,
The task appointed me, but lo -- how the others react!

This my arrest, then, is a watershed, a winnowing.
I alone am left, even now a widowed king,
This scourging, this mocking seem small to compare
With the loss of love -- the double-cross I bear...

Alone ... but I am not alone, not yet, and then but a time
Condensing all believer's eternity of hell, but I'm
Ready now for that, for I've tasted the option,
Dutiless, careless, loveless men -- I'll buy their adoption.

And helpless, I will help more than ever they did or could,
Broken I will bind up as no doctor would
Heartlessly killed, I revive and unharden.
Arrested and punished, I will free and fully pardon.

HEAVEN DROPPED THE BABY

Even before mankind formally declared itself God
And approved the murder of babies, especially before
      birth,
There was occasional cause to consider divine love fraud,
Some excuse to doubt grace ran things on earth.

Every time a baby died, before or after delivery,
Doctors looked helpless and ministers got shivery.
"Higher purpose" and "divine plan" rang a little hollow,
And arguments syllogistic got a bit hard to follow.

The one apologetic that seems to console toward hope,
Aside from raging or despair, or alcohol or dope,
Is that God became a man and felt as we do maybe,
When he himself was born, and himself the dropped baby.

CLOSED EYES

Children in arms we feared to see their eyes dissolve,
Those great lucid lamps of light and love be shuttered,
And cease to signify.

Our own eyes were even more mysterious to us --
How they obliterated and created all reality
In a mere blink.

We fought the closing of our own, but found it harder
To accept the closing of those others.

No longer often in arms, we have learned to accept
The end of sight, life in shuttered dreams --
Accept, except...

When those we love close their eyes,
Those great lucid lamps of light and love
Which cannot cease to signify.

NO RUNT IN THE LITTER

Rural wisdom has little room for the ugly debate
Waged by urban philosophers about death as fate
Rightfully considered as the prerogative of men,
To be decided democratically and administered when
Convenient to the greater happiness of others,
The recipient is assumed glad thus to serve his brothers).

Although tales of bare survival are frequently told,
No rural sage, though his tales make blood run cold,
Draws the point that mankind lives like a crowd in a boat,
Where some must drown others so that some may stay afloat.

No the rural sage tells homely tales in which men fail,
Men fall, and men feel hemmed in, or short of bail.
But men are in it together, be the battle ever so bitter.
None is cast out, none abandoned -- no runt in the litter.

PUT IT OUT OF ITS MISERY

It took no philosophical education or logical regime to
        sharpen up
My wits enough to hear a hollow ring (when I was a young
        pup)
In that expression applied to unwanted pet, a litter, or crowd
        of
Undesireable four-legged infants. I knew the misery out of
Which they were being put, not their own, nor misery no
        doubt --
Just inconvenience. How is it now it's babies we put out?

TIME TO KILL

David on the rooftop had time to kill,
Time the murderer sloped along his sight,
By way of the washroom on Uriah's roof,
A woman's body, and a whoop-it-up night.

Time to kill hangs on America's hands:
Time to myself, time to rest, time stands
Still; then rushes on; clock hands spin:
Time-to-go-out soon time-to-come-in.

Time is the miser's irretrievable craving,
The substance sought by all and everyone,
But beyond all and anyone's saving.
Time is the watchman that shines his torch

61.

Into every window, every bedroom and porch
And reveals what has happened there,
Who's cowers behind the facade.
Time is the foreman in the factory of God.

But we fool ourselves once in a while,
Now and then, occasionally
And think time ours to use, to spend
Or patiently -- to kill.

Then it is that like David's frantic hands
Ours reach for other lives to spend
To satisfy our demands:
A husbands', a wifes', perhaps a child's unborn.
Time to kill become killing time
Becomes a long time to mourn.

ANGELS OF PROMISE AND DOOM

The angels who came to Abram with the promise
Wended their way to Sodom with its doom.
Not all his rhetorical efforts
Or compassion dispelled the gloom
Hanging sulphurious over the cities of the plain,
Soon to be distilled in destruction and pain.

Dual citizens find it hard at that final hour
Decreed by cities for deciding which to shun;
To claim the other, embrace it's rights and power:
To separate to integrate, to be torn into one.
So we citizens of a nation dark death shrouded
Mourn and argue with God, be it ever so beclouded.

But whence from hence we know not,
Ninevah or Gomorrah, tomorrow.
Can his distant promises suffice
To assuage our brooding sorrow?

STARE DECISIS

The old astrologers were starry deciders:
Analyzing what was fixed by fatal decree
As now our magistrates view high court decisions
And hand down the judgments on you and me.

But no star's so fixed God can't let it fall
Nor any judge so high God won't judge all.

RUNNING STOP SIGNS
To a woman considering aborting her baby
(written with Kimiko Trott Nabors)

Those bright red signs do not compel you --
Not at first anyway. They only tell you
Somebody in authority, someone who counts,
Wants something of you he's willing to announce.

You can run one, you can run fifteen,
You can run a hundred -- it's yet to be seen
How many can be run how many different ways
With how many friends for how many days.

But if you run this one, no matter how fast,
The red reminder won't just flash past --
It will long echo -- in pursuing feet --
Footsteps of the child who was crossing the street.

THE PATHOLOGIST

The Pathologist is at home in his lab
Examining parts that have gone bad.
He tells other physicians what went wrong
With liver and lights that don't get along.

But what went wrong with these arms,
These legs, this head, and torso, once whole?
And can anyone diagnose the pathology
Of this organ, the human soul?

THE HOLLOW WOMEN

We are the hollow women,
Larger than life,
Scraped out and scrapped up
By currette and knife.

We are the hollow women
Empty within,
Lighter than a feather . . .
Hollow wo<u>myn.</u>

ABIGAIL BADORF - IN MEMORIAM

Abigail Elizabeth
Ordained by the laying on of hands:
The yet to be born by the elders'--
The unseen by the whole visible church --

And secretly while machines declared a tangle,
    By Greatest Knitter's hands of all.

    Large prayers were answered,
    Granting us a working week
Before you went home to prepare for your family,
    Leaving us too long to long, and to conclude
    Some of the best are women preachers.

            Destined for death
            Come to die,
            Proclaiming Christ
            In softest sigh.

NO ACCIDENT

We have spent billions, will spend trillions more
To prevent those awful murders perpetrated by spore,
By amoeba or virus or extreme weather --
Natural agents of death we oppose altogether.
But thousands perished in manmade clysm,
Are quite all right, safe syllogism --
Death in plane, hospital, train or car,
Ship, bridge, or skyscraper -- these are
Only the price of progress we opine,
We are happy to pay (if the death's not mine).
We don't so much mind wholesale death
As death out of our own control.
We're happy to bury half the race
As long as we've dug the hole.

PARASITOLOGY

A parasite is a living creature
That feeds on you,
Disregards your voice,
Its distinctive feature.
It takes your life
Little by little,
Without your choice.

You can go to a doctor
To have it removed,
The parasite,
That in you has proved
It's definition,
Caused disruption,
Sapping your life,
Incorporate corruption.

But remember all
Your life depends
On father, mother,
Brother, friends;
So if you won't be used,
Not support
This child of yours,
It's no parasite you abort.

Indeed you conceived it,
Invited it's life,
That was your choice.
Where, under the knife,
Is any vote or voice
For this human mite?

Who devours whom?
Which the parasite?

MUTUAL CONSENT

They say you are the key.
Acts that would otherwise bestial be
Becomes a sacrament;
That which differs insubstantially,
A crime, or else best time
Best spent in full charity.
From most injured victim to victim none.
From unspeakable evil to no harm done.
And yet how sadly well I know
How sorely I am often assaulted
By own consent tossed to and fro,
Left scarred by him who can hardly be halted.
Let Donne not his "ravish me" repent --
I, too, need more than mutual consent.

PREACHING TO PILES OF BONES

Every Sunday I preach to bones
Stacked awkwardly in their chairs,
Leaning precariously on their walkers.
Bones poorly connected by ligaments
And poorly clothed in rancid flesh.
But when I prophesy the bones stand
Towering and magnificently clothed
In new flesh and exquisite glory
Before the wheeling central throne --
They preach to me, a mighty army
And arm me to go out and preach
All week to my own pile of bones.

WE ARE THE HOLLER MEN

We are the silent screamers,
Mouths stretched wide in showmanship.
We are the loudmouthed louts
With catcalls and with crowing lips.
Exhausted we, our paucity,
Pomposity, bombosity,
-- Monstrosities:
Gorillas beating on our chests,
Lions roaring without meaning.
We are the holler men,
Crying coarsely cant and keening.

DEATHBED WITH A FUTURE

Either an absurdity,
An insane disjunction,
Or miraculous hope,
Result of some unction
Not in evidence;
Not scientific,
Not susceptible to proof
According to any specific
We see, taste, measure, test.
Yet a deathbed with a future
Would be best.

INCONVENIENCES LIKE BIRTH
(At Hazel's Advent)

When life is interrupted
By inconveniences like birth,
We grope for unaccustomed dress –
Adaptation. The dirth
Of calculation and inadequate
Degree of complaining
Can only be due,
(By way of explaining)
To being but half-awake,
Still as they who dream,

In which condition things
Are not what they seem --
While our sensible self says
'The game was interrupted for a scrimmage' –
Feels almost imposed upon by God,
This new person in his image.

JE REGRET

I regret I did not say what I knew I should have said.
I regret I did not do what I said I would. The dead,
Held they tribunals, would me a traitor hold.
I regret I've grown no wiser although I have grown old.
I regret I knew so many needs and gave so few alms
I regret the things I thought instead, illusionary balms.
I wish I could give the million smiles, strangled by my lips.
I regret I pitied petty me, and not those with true
          hardships.
I regret . . .and you are false who say I hadn't ought.
I regret so much regrettable in deed and word and thought,
And if there were no Savior desperate to take my sin,
I would regret forever the hell I belong in.

FROM UNDER THE RUBBLE

We are survivors, but our biggest trouble –
We can't agree about the rubble.

We can't agree what can be used,
Wonder what must be refused.

Not lone survivors, though alone each wonders,
What kind of rubble we're crawling from under.

What kind of rubble, from what kind of disaster,
What catastrophe we're living after.

What diseases, what radiation,
Deeply infects this broken nation.

Where's ground zero, where's the good fruit and
Who are the zombies, who the mutants?

There's rubble all around us, we do agree
There's been something very like World War III,

But what kind of pick and what kind of shovel,
Will we use to sort through all of this rubble?

IDEOLOGY

I've been doing this crossword puzzle
For many and many a day.
I put my favorite word in first
And now have got almost half-way –
But somehow few of the clues
Clear though at times they seem,
Yield me further words to fit
Within my own heart's scheme.
As sure as I am what I hold is sooth,
Somehow it gets in the way of truth.

FIFTY MILLION VOICES

You speak of babies voices --
I hear monstrous ovens ring
With the hollow haunted chorus
Fifty million sing –
Not sing, but wail, not wail but whisper,
Not whisper but faintly moan.
Fifty million voices –
An infinitive drone.
They are discounted, doubted, quite forgot --
Only fifty million voices --
Not heard but heard not.
Yet far, far from a silence --
Fifty million empty sighs,
Witnesses against us

'Til all wrath dies.
God not only hears them
But answers their chorus
With his effectual curse --
Savior, pray for us!

BLOOD TALK

The bloody-breasted robin,
The bloody-taloned hawk,
The bloody-muzzled coyote –
If only blood could talk.

Could talk of stretch and snap,
Could talk of snatch and pierce
Could talk of crush and tearing --
Then blood talk would be fierce.

Fierce blood takes the worm,
Takes the robin in its claws,
Clasps the hawk in its firm jaws
And brings the wolf to term.

IT IS FINISHED . . .

The creation –
The race –
The nation –
The disgrace.

NOT PERSONIFICATION

It is personification
To speak of a mountain
As though it were a man;
To call a ship a lady;
Attribute human emotions to a cat;
Or human thoughts to a rodent.
It is personification
To treat as human the sun or moon,
A lion or a flea,
Things vast or infinitesimal.
It is not personification
To call a baby a baby,
Nor is it merely a pathetic fallacy –
Rather a tragic one –
To call it anything else.
It is de-personification,
Denying God in his image,
And ones very self.

DREAM OF CHILDREN

Moses had a dream for Israel –
It was the children entering in.
How is it our American dream
Has no place for the children?
Rev. King spoke of his dream,
A vision for those yet unborn.
How is it then it is especially these
We have come so to scorn?

THIRD GENERATION

What you collect,
What you come to worship,
Your children will invoke
In more fervent sacrifices –
Placing their children in turn
On the altars
Heated to a glowing heat
For incineration.

SECTION FOUR: JAIL POEMS

GOOD-BYE TO KEY ROAD
Key Road Prison, Atlanta 1988

Good-bye to the remnants of old slavery,
Good-bye to servants with overseer's hearts,
Good-bye to the distant Georgia hills --
Where I would have sat and wept.
Good-bye to the little knot of converts,
And the yet-to-believe male prostitutes.
But my good-bye involves no crucifixion --
It is pure resurrection . . .
Someone else is paying the bail.
Hurry after me!

THE TANK

When we enter this jail we're thrown in the tank,
Regardless of crime or connection or rank,
Where some stand, some sit on the concrete floor,
As some complain less and others more.
Some light up or bum a smoke
As someone cracks a jailhouse joke.
Some silent, pray; some silent, no more;
Some listen carefully at the door

For steps or news or a familiar voice.
When lunch is brought in, few rejoice.
Some come from court bearing a sentence,
Others hope their new-found repentance
Will soften the judges stony heart,
Others know to play the well-worn part.
Some go from here to a narrow cell,
Others leave for a world never loved so well.

WHICH-ILITATION

If the object is to rehabilitate, facilitate
A changed life, a sense of repentance and renewal,
Washing worth worth redeeming from muck,
Then two things need be sharp distinguished
And all means given to God
To separate in heart, mind, and fact,
Good from evil.

But if the object is debilitation, maceration
Of unworthy human souls and lives,
That they may be flushed without resistance
Down garbage disposals and toilets of a society
Which believes in real good and evil
Only as self is good, others otherwise,
Then current techniques are indeed effective --

Flood the injured cells in their cells,
And hurting hearts with corruption,
Until the distinction between self and sin
Is utterly lost. Bring in bribery, drugs,
And a constant flow of pornographic
And materialistic television and books
To poison every barricaded bit of soul.

Ah, but Christ seeks his prisoners,
In the depths of the offal.

THINGS GO WRONG

In this place things go wrong,
Letters are lost, lines are long,
Doors close, phones go dead,
Guards can't hear, requests go unread.
Despair is the logical soul's conclusion --
Chaos reigns; hope, an illusion
Unless someone tends this jail like a garden,
And waters and weeds, both prisoner and warden;
Unless someone sentence himself life-long
To redeem and teach us to right what's wrong

OUR CELLS

We hate and love these walls of cell,
Cinderblock: glazed, nine courses; painted, seven and half.
The one window, the steel sink and john,
The concrete floor and bunk I sit on.

We hate them because they hold us,
We love them because they're ours.
And when the door trips to allow us
A little less narrowness of scope,
We hesitate to lock the door behind --

As we must to obey orders and protect possessions.
And when this little cave echoes back
Our prayers, our despairs (no penetration)
We curse ourselves in like echo fashion.

Or when letters and phone free our voices
To fly beyond the visible fence,
We bless ourselves by faith.

Often the letters are not answered
Or the phone busy.
Sometimes the prayers go furthest.

We hate our cells because they are ours,
We love them because they hold us.

CONCEPTIONS and images :

BALLAD OF THE LOST PRO-LIFE PRISONERS
(written together with Chet Gallagher)

A tisket, a tasket, Atlanta blew a gasket
Mayor Young who bossed it, he had a list but lost it.
He lost it, he lost it, he had a list but lost it
Hold on ----- Hold on –
Keep your eyes on the prize – Hold on.

MARBLE FLOORS

The intolerant squares in these courthouse halls
March in perfect order without variation or question.

The one upon which I now stand
Is the only one with any bearing to my eyes.

The others leap away in quick diminishing
Into complete insignificance.

But my heart's eyes see the lines parallel --
Not converging -- and extending into eternity.

SENTENTIOUSNESS

And low his deliberate phrases roll
Slowly stifling the flow of his soul.

JURY SELECTION

If you cannot set aside your opinions:
If you cannot empty your heart;
If you cannot deny what you certainly know --
Then you cannot sit on the jury.

But if you can be this impartial,
What opinion have you of the Judge?

THE SENSITIVE CHRISTIAN

"I couldn't send a pastor to jail",
She said, thus excusing herself from the jury:
By which act she most certainly
Sentenced the pastor to jail.

TIP STAFF

Moses, too, was a judge over many,
Had an extensive staff,
Used its tip with power.
But when he trusted it --
Trusted himself rather than God,
His impaired judgment fell on him.

LAW OFFICER

Rather than weaken the prosecution's case,
The objective officer resigns himself
To agree to remembering what never was --
To deny all law as well as his office.

MUTUAL RESPECT

We have a relationship of mutual respect
The abortionist told the court
In reference to other "respectable" pro-lifers.
Which was a lie, but may serve as shibboleth

For those in dialogue with the world,
The flesh and the devil.

JOHN THE B IN PRISON

He knew the system couldn't be trusted,
And had long divorced himself from it, except
As the Lord sent him with rebukes and prophecy.

That was all it took to get him into jail,
(No doubt Herod legalled it up with an injunction or
    two)
Where Salome was to resolve all his doubts for him.

But meanwhile doubt he did, as I do,
Sitting here listening to the drone of injustice,
And the complacent legalism of absolute relativism.

He knew God's promises fulfilled: had seen, heard,
But churned with existential doubt.
This feels like vanity, Lord, here in this void.

John the B. sent messengers to ask,
As I do these, Lord,
As I do these.

INNOCENT UNTIL PROVEN GUILTY

This supposed bulwark of our great nation
Has become a ghastly, ill-proportioned joke.
The legal dogma derived from the doctrine of sin,
An article now denied, now blasphemy bespoke.
An accused man was presumed innocent, not because he
Was thought sinless, or truthful or blame-free,
But because his accusers, and all officers of law
Were assumed to have, as he had, the original flaw
Of fallen men, self-serving, truth-of-God-deniers,
As likely as the accused to prove to be liars.
Now the incredible doctrine that men are good
(And growing better)
Binds the court to antithesis, to presumed guilt,
Like a fetter.
For if mankind is evolving, taken as a whole,
The few are wrong, not the many,
Not society, but the sole.
The law is presumed flawless,
The judge is presumed all-wise,
The police all pure and honest,
The Christian guilty in all eyes.

BEYOND A REASONABLE DOUBT

"To find the defendants guilty you must be convinced beyond
reasonable doubt. A reasonable doubt is a doubt such that if a
reasonable person encountered it in the course of his affairs it
would cause him to hesitate."

Reasonable sounds so reasonable. Eve thought so, too.
Enlightenment man worships reason, wants the same from
     you.
Will you make reason the basis for your justice and law,
Or bow, admitting to God reason's fatal flaw?

Any doubt may be reasoned... Any reason may be doubted.

THE BURDEN OF THE PROOF

For the purposes of a criminal court the prosecution
Bears the burden of proof - in theory if not practice:
Must demonstrate beyond reasonable doubt
Guilt in terms of what law and what fact is.
But the burden of proof in another court
And the penalty each will pay
Will rest strictly with the defense --
All will lose who are *pro se*.

LE COURT C'EST MOI

Louis the Fourteenth -- that epitome of absolute
Monarchs (who among us are usually cursed),
Is said to have been more absolute
Than England's James, the First,
As evidenced in those famous words,
Which come down to us as a saw:
"The state? I am the state,""L'etat c'est moi."
Without arguing the virtues of dem- or - mon-ocracy,
One might suggest there's more than a little hypocrisy
In judicial declarations regarding American law,
Of absolute authority -- "Le court c'est moi."

CONSPIRACY CHARGES

According to the judge one is a criminal conspirator
If he or she enters an agreement, not necessarily explicit
To commit a crime and any one party thus agreed
Then performs an act that is the crime indeed.
The essence, says the judge, is a common understanding.
An accomplice acts to promote or facilitate a crime.
Which standards if Christ should apply to his Bride,
Makes us conspirators and accomplices in infanticide.

HARD WORDS

Being civil is sometimes God's calling and God's best,
But mene, mene, tekel, parsum: we've failed the test
Of those other times, myriad have they been,
When to be quiet or civil was nothing short of sin.
Soft words, peace, peace, are hell's oil, the devil's grease
With which true peace is slid from the way,
And quietly wrecked so that no one can say,
Just when it happened, or if it happened it all --
Except an Elijah, a Jesus, or a Paul --
Who were much less civil than (never nice as)
We who disapprove of all verbal devices
With weight and edge, that strike, that cut or
Refuse to melt like our words of butter.
We speak so, not in love -- how harsh is a Father --
Rather simply because we'd rather not bother.

THE FACTS OF THE CASE

The judge solemnly order the jury to avoid all news,
All print or broadcasts of views of the case,
To resort themselves solely to the case presented
In court and that wholly -- the witnesses, the evidence,
If only the church would do so we could rest our defense.

FAILURE TO IDENTIFY

Although they'd scarcely gone out when back they came
With "guilty", none of the jury so much as knew my name.

DEGRADATION LOOKING GOOD

Few if any of us refuse to know that scorn may be borne,
May be transmitted by air by less than a glare, by a look,
And even perchance, by a glance.

Where as children almost from the carriage, we disparaged
In open, intemperate epithet and tone, we have so grown,
That now our bile, often wears a smile.

The essence of insult is dehumanization, degradation
Of other full and worthy human beings to things,
Bidding them die by annihilating eye.

The eye is not a mere organ of sense. Its propensity
To perceive is but one of its tasks. It sends and asks,
Touches and recoils, agrees, foils.

Although modesty is a lost virtue, now rumored to hurt,
It's maxim that eyes touch, said much, much more
Than optometry's lore knows or admits.

Certainly.

If eyes touch, then a glance may be a blow. We know
This a convention, but there is little mention made
As such, not much, of another kind of touch.

None of us want to be things despised, but prized?
We recognize and resist a look that rejects as it inspects,
But learn we must to mistrust lust.

And even when lusts' objects have learned to spurn it;
That it degrades, treats beating heart like meat mart,
Those whose eyes burn are slow to learn.

For eyes do more than see, touch and send, they reflect,
And send back the dot and dash, the soul unshuttering
        flash,
What they first sent begin to believe, now receive.

So the man turning the outrageous, angel-of-light pages
Of the pornographic book, like a welder at a mirror,
Blinds his own eyes with the sear flame.

His gaze lights no paper, but like the bolder raper
Of a woman, made for him un-person, he may be sure
Something is consumed, fades to ash in the hot flash.

The eyes are soul gates, both release and let in,
Sin comes and goes, ebbs and flows, washes the shores
Both outer and inner, erodes the sinner.

Degradation is not a one-way transaction, the active faction,
Whether desiring or hating, is thus always driving itself
Toward the soul-dead state it sees the other's fate.

KILLDEER'S CRIES

Killdeer's cries are the only calls pierce these impenetrable
    walls.
The mother killdeer drags her wing to lead the predator from
    her young.
We stood, arms limp, in front of mothers, predators of their
    own babies...
And so these walls. "Kee-ee, kill-ll" cuts through them and
    our hearts.
The Bird Man of Alcatraz, like most prisoners loved what was
    free:
Went, moved freely beyond these walls: we see the wild geese
Circle, seeking, as we hear the killdeer.
Somewhere in this prison today, a young man lies in his cell,
A young man who tortured another to death.
Do those cries echo in his cell as the killdeer's echo in mine?
Not even the heavy machinery sounds, heater motors and
    blaring TV
Drown out the plaintiff, the sorrowing cry against the
    destroyer,
The destroyers, and the walls.

PRISON ROOFER

He's inside the compound, inside the razor wire --
Seem's to be a prisoner with us, only a little higher,
But he comes and goes at will, passes by the guards.
The tapping of his hatchet signals across the yard.

Why come here unless compelled?
What leak in a prison roof
Draws the workman to this jail
Who could remain aloof?

CHEWING DIAMONDS

Chewing diamonds, crystalline truth
Stronger than jaw or tongue or tooth --
A stream of bright spikes, spectacular:
Awful aliments, original, oracular.

To a throat used to gruel,
To a stomach stuffed with starch,
This meal of shining burning is a cruel
Ice blizzard in March.

Can my molars and eye-teeth survive it --
Can my entrails hold adamants in?
Or will they pierce and kill me --
Grave stones engraving within?

And yet, this meal over which I mutter
Converts my soul to a diamond cutter!

YESTERDAY'S SALT

Isn't yesterday's salt enough!
Haven't I lightened and leavened heaven's rising sufficiently
Without today being savory?
Lord, how I hate this antinomy
That when I have served best I must still serve thee.
I like to muse upon, to savor (that word again)
The fading grains of conversations past -- rather than fast
In order to prepare a sacrifice today of testimony ready
always.
Can't my yesterday's wise advice, counsel and prayer
Suffice where I am fearful to fail?
Let me tally the tale, taste the fruit...

No, I don't suppose I want to be trodden underfoot.

MUZZLES

That's what Solzhenitsyn called them in the *Gulag*:
These heavy screens on our windows that admit light,
And perhaps a little air, but muzzle sight.
The faithful faithfully agree faith and sight oppose,
But God knows, an incarnation is occasionally needed,
For our lukey faith to be heated, rather than cool.
Thus muzzles are cruel, for the harder one stares,
The more one cares, the less he sees through these.
(Since it strains eyes to tears, one who closely peers
Through a wire hole unclogged, soon tires of staring.)

It is only the uncaring who accomplish the mission,
Unmuzzle sight through motion rather than vision --
Like faith, a puzzle.

MESSAGE IN CRAYON

Because God speaks to me so well,
I try to speak in kind
With ceremonies, hymns and prayers,
With verses poorly rhymed.

As my children bring me scribbled scraps
Lined out in careful crayon,
I labor elaborate efforts at
"I love you, Daddy," in pen.

LOOKING AT THE LIGHT

I look into the light
Despite the fact no sense I make --
    (all images are lost)
The glass is quite opaque
    (with chemical frost)

Not even the sun
Makes its daily run distinct to view,
But always new, the light streams in
And scours up sin. It lifts my heart
To start again and keep on looking
Further than I see --
Into the light.

BREAKING FAST

On the crossbar of the plastic tray
The fellow inmate set the styrofoam cup
Of red juice with which I broke my fast.

SUICIDE WATCH

If you demonstrate depression
Or answer a question wrong,
Indicating any ambivalence
About lasting here too long,
They take away your clothes
(Clothes can make a rope),
Dress you rudely in paper rags,
Make you look like a dope,

And carefully observe you
(At least for a day or two)
So that if you murder anyone --
At least it won't be you.
Stripped and embarrassed,
Those on suicide watch stand
Awkwardly about,
Unsure about the demands
Or their dementia's dimensions
Amidst a time and nation
Less obscure in its intentions.

PRISON BREAKFAST

My mother told me eat your mush
There are people starving in China.
My mother told me, eat your eggs,
There are people starving in Africa.
My mother told me eat you food.
I'm sorry, Mom, I don't mean to be rude,
But no matter what you said,
Here I'd rather starve – in bed!

I NEED A WINDOW

I need to see out -- a window, though small,
Is a necessity of heart. Though these bars gall
Me and little cell constrain, a sight
Of the greater world keeps off soul's night;
I strain for a glimpse of sky, a few feet of earth
To see, to be to me a joy: to view the day's birth,
I need -- a sunrise, moon, or a star or two. . .
Failing these a sidewalk or brick wall will do.

I need to see even a razor wire fence
To get my bearings, calculate my position.
In this place of confinement and indecision
I need further visions from which to make sense.

GLOBAL WARMING

Global warming is one of our little terrors,
Based on pop-sci gurus, and old errors.
Though it be founded on delusion,
Nevertheless I believe the conclusion:

Though ice-caps not melt, oceans not swell;
Though earth not subside under watery hell,
In other terms tremendous floods may start --
With just a little warming, a small change of heart.

97.

THEIR JOYS

In prison we do not resent
The joys that come to others --
What belongs to them
Is so clearly delineated:
Meals, uniforms, cups, spoons -- and visitors
Are theirs, not ours,
And so we wake them when they are asleep,
Or help them get ready to receive their blessings.
Their releases, too, are theirs alone;
Nor can be other.   Knowing this
We rejoice with them
And look only for that
Which will be ours.

AGRICULTURAL DECISIONS

How do you know whether to harvest, water, sow?
Go into the field, touch the grain in the row.
Study head by head -- is it ready for bread
Or is it green and growing, or shriveled and dead?

HEADHUNTERS

Taking pride like the South Sea headhunter
In the number of trophies they accumulate,
The guards are disappointed
When they come up short

They do a special count then --
Making sure not only of numbers,
But also of names
They have written in their books --
Like another headhunter.

HAVE YOU BEEN TO THE PLACE?

Have you been to the place where the walls are cold,
The windows small and the bosses bold
  --I been there.
Have you been to the place where calls are collect,
They call it corrections though that's not correct
  -- I been there.
Have you been to the place where you lose your mind,
Have you been to the place where the sun don't shine
  -- I been there.
And Jesus been there , too.
Brother he's there for you.

Have you been to the place where the blankets scratch,
Half a smoke is lit with half a strike, half a match
 -- I been there.
Where you drop your load on a cold steel seat,
Reminds you of some of the stuff you eat
 -- I been there.
Have you been there where the tough guys snap,
And you're always tired though you always nap
 --I been there.
And Jesus been there, too.
Brother he's there for you.

Have you been to the place where strange people meet,
Where you read the Bible or a new charge sheet,
 -- I been there.
Have you been there where the doors are steel,
And you're so on edge , you don't know how to feel,
 --I been there.
Have you been there where the nights conspire
To make you meditate on the razor wire
 -- I been there,
And Jesus been there, too.
Brother, he's there for you --
He's been there.
Right now, He's there for you!

APRIL GRASS

The grass inside the razor wire is lush
And studded with dandelions
Densely springing toward the sun.
The blades and flowers are wild, uncut,
And richly endowed,
Fulfilling little of their calling --
Except to make me wonder
From my cell.

CRAZY TOM

Crazy Tom freaked out and lost it,
Started yelling at the cops;
Told the one who bossed it,
"You're arresting the wrong ones!
Listen you fools!
They kill babies in there."
-- He didn't play by the rules.

We took him aside and said, "Tom, my friend,
This yelling and screaming, this anger must end,
We are doing a rescue, peaceful, and prayerful",
But his eyes were still wild, his expression baleful.

So next time we told him nothing about it --
Afraid he'd freak out again and shout at
The police, the women, the pro-abort crowd,
And say those things again -- out loud.

Something about Tom and Tom's reaction,
Moves my heart more than a fraction.
Crazy Tom freaked out -- out of bound-ed
Or did sane Tom see truth and act sanely astounded?

SHAKEDOWN

When we were taking it easy,
Dozing on the last meal,
The gates opened, a squad came in
And shook us up a great deal --

All of my possessions,
My person, desk, bunk, and box
They searched for any contraband,
I might have got past the locks.

You never know when they may come
To search you and your cellie.
You anxiously search your memory,
Concerning drugs, weapons -- or jelly.

Your heart, your mind and conscience
Get shaken down as well --
Or will be -- by Someone
Able to shake down to hell.

ENOUGH EVIDENCE TO CONVICT YOU

Would you like to catechize Washington's wraith?
Or determine the measure of old Abe's faith?
First tell posterity, should it happen to pick you,
Have you left any evidence here to convict you?

Do you find Bob Dylan hard to follow?
Are you clear of the mud of the TV wallow?
Claim which famous name believes nothing to stick to?
But does your record show anything to convict you?

Are you tired of doom prophets demanding action?
Do you favor repentance -- by a mere fraction?
Would you go to the lions, if they only licked you?
Could anyone find any clue to convict you?

RAZORWIRE HALOES
(Bergen County Jail, March 1997)

The halogen lights
Burn the razor wire
Into haloes;
Generate sharp brilliances
Against the black sky
Narrow through the window slit --
Slit by the razor wire

Cut by the the arc lights
Into a wound
As wide as eternity
Through the wall of
This unclean cell.

BORN DEAD

I was born dead.
She who bore me thought it was my resurrection,
Thought I was the stone rolled from the tomb
Where she long lingered.
And she was not alone.
I was born to bear the ghost --
To walk again from their Valley of Dry Bones;
And so I was born a dual character --
A character in a duel,
War-torn embodiment of two adversaries --
I who . . . and he who . . .
With the one great question --
Hanging over our contest --
Who would live ?
And I live -- though I was born dead.
He who never died for her, is dead in me.
And I who was born dead, I am alive.

THIS CHILD

This life, this child
Is one on whom God smiled,
Knit it bit by bit
In the womb, a composite
Of infinite care and intense love.
None knows what He's thinking of
When he makes one thus – this we know
He loves these best of all below.

In his image they are spun,
Bought in blood, one by one.
Each unique with mystery plan –
No other woman, no other man
Like her, like him – not one
So precious that he'd give his son,
An infinite moment his own reviled
For this life, this child
-- and smiled!

Made in the USA
Middletown, DE
03 July 2015